A Naturalist's Eye:
Writings from Puget Sound Country

Janet Partlow

2014

Introduction

In 1994 I became a volunteer staff writer for the <u>Green Pages</u>, which is a publication of the South Puget Environmental Education Clearing House in Olympia, Washington. This environmental newspaper is a stronghold of independent journalism in southern Puget Sound. It provides in-depth coverage of many environmental issues and politics and the local nature watchers rely on it for excellent coverage of the topics close to our hearts.

I decided to share my time & writing, thinking it would be great to add my voice as a naturalist, helping people connect even more deeply to the same environment that they were attempting to preserve & protect. I wrote for <u>Green Pages</u> for three years.

These writings were influenced by a few things: during these years my husband Glen and I were caretakers of a twenty acre property at Trosper Lake south of Olympia. This land is featured in some of these columns.

I also worked on the one thousand acre campus of The Evergreen State College in Olympia. Some of my best nature experiences happened while walking through the woods from the parking lot to the building I worked in.

This book is a collection of writings from that time and those places.

Janet Partlow

Fall

Humans Once Followed the Patterns of Nature

We have it in our genes to be nature watchers.

We are animals, though we have largely forgotten our animal ways. There was a time when the pattern of the stars, the rhythm of weather and wind, of tides and streams was indelibly imprinted on our daily lives.

Once we were able to wake in the dawn and note the position of the stars and know exactly the day of the year. We smelled the salty wind coming off the estuary and knew what the weather held for that day. We studied the patterns of leaf fall, bent shreds of grass, faint pressure marks in the springy moss by the stream and knew what animals had passed that way in the night.

We knew of spring's coming by the call of the Chinook wind, long before the first green shoots of cattail pushed their way through the bottom of the marsh. We knew of the stealthy approach of the hunting cat by the changes in the calls of the birds in the trees. Our lives were intimately tied to all of nature. We learned nature's lessons, or we did not survive.

We are all nature watchers.

We live now by the clock which tells us when it is time to get up, by the newspaper which tells us when the tide will change. We watch television to tell us the weather, though I assure you that you can be as accurate as any weatherman by spending five minutes looking at the clouds and the direction of the wind.

We know of the movements of wild animals only by the flattened remains along our highways. The rain is an enemy, to be bested by newer and improved rain gear. The wind is a problem, threatening to topple the last big Douglas fir in the neighborhood. We have gotten rid of our predators; when the story of a grizzly attack makes the rounds, we in terror demand that all grizzlies need to be moved or shot.

This column is a call to wake up, to start looking again at the world around us, to be reconnected with the animals that we are.

As animals we learned the ancient ways of living in this world; as evolved humans we have chosen to leave those ways behind us.

I believe it is time for us to reclaim a critical part of our heritage. We need to learn again to live fully in the present, to use all our animal senses and to experience the natural world as our species has done for generations.

Owls at Trosper Lake

A few years ago, we became caretakers for a twenty acre wetland at Trosper Lake in Tumwater. This was a beautiful place, with a swamp and seasonal stream running through old-growth conifers to a beaver-engineered lake. It was during this time we became very acquainted with owls.

Shortly after we moved to the place in late August, we went out on the deck for some stargazing. Suddenly, out of the woods some twenty feet off the deck came a horrific, strangled screaming high up in the trees. The screaming voice flew in a nearby tree and continued shrieking at us. We were flabbergasted at the sound and not a little freaked out.

After some consideration, we thought it must be a screech owl but in fact our Western Screech Owls do not screech. We checked an audiotape on owl calls and realized it must be a Barn Owl, making its alarm/threat call. Certainly it both alarmed and threatened us!

It was a few months later that we started to hear a different owl hooting regularly at dusk. It sat in a tree outside our bedroom window and gave a quiet, rolling series of hoots that had the cadence of a dropped ping-pong ball, pinging faster and faster as the bounce shortens. This is the normal hoot of the Western Screech Owl.

It became a regular part of our evening ritual: from January through April the bird called almost every evening. These owls were our close neighbors throughout our two years at Trosper Lake and we came to love their company.

In our last year at Trosper Lake, a new owl moved into the neighborhood. On Thanksgiving morning we were sleeping in, enjoying the novelty of a day off. But our sleep was rudely interrupted by a murder of crows (a large flock) shrieking, hollering, caterwauling and flying erratically in and out of one tall Western Cedar near the house.

This is typical mobbing behavior of crows and they direct it towards their mortal enemies: hawks and owls. Hawks usually respond to such pressure by taking off for a quieter neighborhood, but owls will usually sit tight. The mobbing went on for a couple of hours, so I suspected we had a Great Horned Owl newly come to the land.

Sure enough, a few nights later, we heard the low, powerful hoots of a Great Horned echoing through the wetland. We quickly bundled up in outdoor gear and walked to the lake, tracking the owl call.

Though we could not see the owl, we got as close to the sound as we dared. The owl high up in the fir tree near the lake called out to the night. The sound slithered down my spine and gave me the shivers. It probably had the same effect on all the small mammals and birds in the vicinity.

Great Horned Owls are very territorial and do not generally tolerate the presence of any other owl. A couple of weeks after the first owl hoots, we found the evidence of a freshly killed Barn Owl. The feathers had been plucked out, which is typical of the way a bird of prey prepares its meal. We suspected the Great Horned Owls had put an end to our resident Barn Owl.

Because these owls blend so well into the darkness of the night, we rarely actually saw them. But their songs, hooting through the dark woods, became an important part of our life at Trosper Lake. Sometimes late in the night I was pulled out of a deep sleep by the sound of a Great Horned Owl, claiming its territory and its mate

Like the calls of night watchmen, the hooting of the owls gave me a sense of comfort and well-being. Lulled by the song of owls, I pulled the blanket more closely around me and slipped back into sleep.

Wild Geese

It was late in October, on a day that tasted of fall: wood smoke and Gravenstein apples, autumn leaves and salt water fog off the bay. The fog was laid out in thick billows across the sky; I looked up and saw a skein of Canada Geese, honking across the last days of summer, cutting a V in the sky as they headed south for winter.

Later that week I drove past a pasture where two horses grazed placidly. In the same field a flock of Canada geese had taken a break from migration and had touched down to rest. Some geese had their heads curved down, cropping away at the rough marsh plants. Others were taking a snooze, their capacious chests nestled deep into the grass, heads tucked away under their wings. Still others were on guard: two in particular had their necks straight up, heads swiveling, dark eyes alert and searching all quarters for danger. This is a typical afternoon for Canada Geese: a little snack, an early nap and always, someone on guard caring for the flock and protecting all from predators.

I have other memories of Canada geese. Some years ago I moved back to Olympia after many years away. The town and I had both changed a great deal and I knew very few people in those first solitary months. Often I walked down to Capitol Lake with a bag of cracked corn to feed the geese. (This was in the time before we knew that geese in our area should not be given supplemental feed: it disrupts their migration patterns.)

I visited the geese regularly that winter and I believe they came to know me. I made a point of approaching them slowly, careful to respect them and their natural wariness of humans. I stood and dribbled corn around myself then waited very quietly, keeping my eyes away from theirs. Slowly over weeks the geese decided to trust me, moving closer, always with an eye out for a sudden movement. I found that in order to be near the geese I needed a quiet, meditative state of mind and a still body.

After several visits, it seemed as if the geese came to know and accept me as a extended member of the tribe (the corn helped!) I vividly remember one day at the lake, looking over the water with Canada Geese all around me. They were picking corn off my shoes and out of my hand, accepting my presence among them for nearly an hour. I felt as if I was an honored guest to the flock; for a time the geese and I were friends. In an odd way, they provided a kind of friendship and support in those early lonely months that I would never have expected to find outside of the company of humans.

And so now, in this October, the year is drawing to a close. The Canada Geese are taking flight, making their way to greener and warmer pastures. I look in the sky and see their flight; I remember my friends and send them blessings on their journey as they are winging their way south to their winter home.

Fungal Fascination

So one autumn morning I woke up and suddenly I was in love with mushrooms.

People often ask me how I got interested in a particular aspect of natural history. Mostly I answer by scratching my head and saying " I dunno". It just seems to happen: buried interests suddenly spring up full grown out of my psyche like the fruit of the mycelia from the compost pile. That day, the fruit of choice was mushrooms.

I dragooned a friend into going to Ellis Cove creek trail one wet afternoon in November. As we walked along the path we found ourselves increasingly drawn to the life in the decomposing leaf litter.

Fat shrimpy-smelling Russulas thrust their red tops out from the forest duff underneath a Douglas fir tree. Artist's conk shelf fungus rammed itself out from under the bark of a dying tree. Velvety black earth tongue fungi pushed up from the moss and waved at us.

The Hideous Gomphidius, which lives out its slimy life underneath evergreen trees, was prominent in the woods and the slugs were all over them, carving out a neat meal. Orange glops of goo called Witches Butter oozed out from cracks in the trunks of alder trees. Under the pine trees we found a kind of bolete mushroom called a Slippery Jack.

Many animals besides humans like to eat mushrooms. Not only slugs are extraordinarily fond of them, but so too are small mammals. If you look carefully at the caps of mushrooms, you will often see tiny mammal teeth marks nibbled into the edges.

While on the Oregon coast last fall, we saw many red mushrooms of a kind called fly amanita. They grew in large numbers under the Sitka spruce. These amanitas are quite toxic to humans, but the Douglas squirrels love to eat them and do so with impunity.

As we walked along, we saw a lot of bright white stems of mushrooms standing upright in the pale autumn sun, but the caps were gone. It was pretty clear that the squirrels had literally logged off all the amanitas caps and run off in the woods with them.

Another animal that likes mushrooms are flies: they like to lay their eggs in them and the growing larvae then feast on the mushrooms. It's not as surprising as it sounds: mushrooms have a meaty quality to them and insects find that compelling.

Flies are particularly fond of bolete mushrooms. One day Glen brought home a new kind of bolete for us to look at and try to identify. It sat in a bowl on our kitchen table for a couple of days while I waited to find a time to look it up in the book.

It was quite a beautiful bolete, but inedible to humans. Not so to flies. One morning Glen got up and went to the kitchen for breakfast. He noticed the bolete had disappeared. The only thing in the bowl was a lump of brown slime.

Unbelieving, he bent his head closer and noticed that the lump was vibrating. He poked at it and watched masses of white maggots bolt out from the slime and head for safer pastures. The bolete had dissolved into maggot mush.

I have made a point of telling this story to my more squeamish friends, just to watch them squirm. It also ensures that no one wants to come to our kitchen table for awhile, a useful thing in the holiday season!

For those of use who love nature, this kind of thing is endlessly fascinating. Flies and their maggots have a place in the world, as do mushrooms. In this season of cold, the fungi are active underneath the leaves, the grass and deep in the soil, breaking down the decaying products of summer and making the world ready for spring.

Learning from Leaves

As I walk to work each day through the woods that lead from the parking lot, my eyes are caught by the fallen leaves plastered wet against the pavement. I see the cutout forms of alder leaves, dog-toothed along the edges and the big leaf maple leaves, forming a five-lobed leaf twice as big as my hand. The oval egg shapes of Scouler's willow leaves and the small fine-toothed edges of birch from the tree nearby all lie at my feet.

All of these leaves have fallen from the tree, and create tracks like footprints, allowing me to identify the tree long after its leaves have disappeared. Many of these leaves were torn down in winter storms and now rest and rot at the base of the tree, recycling nutrients back into the soil.

Humans generally seem to find these leaves an annoyance. At my workplace, the maintenance staff don ear protectors, strap on leaf blowers and wage an on-going battle to control the leaves. But nature has a different idea. The tree which spent six months building leaves and using them to make and store carbohydrates from the sun's energy also drops those leaves in the soil above its own roots, ensuring that the nutrients will be available in the soil for the next year's growth.

However, the tree cannot "eat" its own leaves whole. It requires an army of intermediaries who break the leaves down and make their nutrients available. For example, the earthworms wake up at night and dig burrows up to the surface where they grab the leaves, dragging them back down into the soil to be munched in safety and later passed on as worm castings.

A wide variety of microscopic animals also play a role. Bacteria, nematodes, fungal mycelia: all are detrivores, breaking the leaf components down into something that can be recycled and used. At the end of the process, the tree gets its leaves back as dissolved minerals in the water it takes in by its own roots. And an entire soil ecosystem is fed and nurtured by the tree's leaves.

Other animals use leaves as well. One year shortly after we moved into a new house our huge apple tree dropped its load of leaves all over the grass. It was a busy time and we didn't get around to raking them up. To our surprise, the leaves attracted a wide variety of ground birds to the yard. That fall varied thrushes, robins and towhees homed in on our backyard. They used their bills to turn the leaves to glean for insects. Their strong legs scratched vigorously at the leaves, hoping to bring a plump tidbit to the surface. Golden-crowned and white-crowned sparrows, song and fox sparrows all lived in our backyard that winter; we often saw them foraging around the leaves.

We also watched an Eastern gray squirrel exploit the leaf resource. It moved from clump to clump, carefully examining under each wet mass for something good to eat. Most likely it was interested in protein: slug eggs, insect larvae, earthworms . Such protein is in short supply in winter and so has a high value as a food resource.

There is one garden bed at our house in which nothing grows well. I think it is time to take a lesson from the leaves. We will put some worm castings from our food bin on the soil, then rake up our neighbor's big leaf maple leaves as a top dressing. Maybe this will attract the worms, the fungi, the bacteria into the garden. And maybe next year, the plants will prosper in a soil built on leaves.

Winter

Watching Like a Hawk

A sharp-shinned hawk has started coming to our bird feeder. I use the term "bird feeder" in the broadest sense of course. We put it in our back yard to attract seed-eater birds. But the predators that like to snack on birds are also attracted to the feeder. Cats for example: in the heat of summer it is not uncommon to look out and see one or two overweight domestic tabbies, sacked out in the shade nearby the feeder, dreaming of the big catch to come.

Hawks are another predator at the bird feeder, but for me a far more welcome one. They are unpredictable in their passage through our area and fascinating to watch.

I remember one cold winter day; I'd stayed home from work because of the heavy snow. I sat in my warm house, near the picture window and watch a large flock of songbirds at my feeder: over 100 evening grosbeaks, pine siskins, towhees, and chickadees all worked busily through the falling snow. Their activity and the noise they made was tremendous and probably drew the attention of the hunting merlin. With a burst of falcon speed, it cut a sharp path through my garden like the curved scythe from which is draws its genus name. It scattered the flock before it in a deadly scramble for cover. The silence at my feeder was deafening for two hours after.

Sharp-shinned hawks used a different strategy. The one I saw recently was an immature bird, learning its trade in urban backyards. This bird was lurking in a wild cherry tree that was surrounded by a thick, concealing privet hedge. I had been sitting out on the back porch for well over an hour and I never knew it was there, fifteen feet away. Nor did one unwary house finch, who chose a moment to pop up from the privet hedge and head for the feeder. The sharp-shinned hawk darted down from its hiding place and seized the finch in its long bird-catching talons. It killed the finch by clenching those dagger like talons around the body, stabbing away into the vital organs.

Then as I watched in shock and fascination, the hawk flew directly over my head, the house finch dangling from its right talons. The hawk pumped its wings to gain elevation over my head and my roof to find a safe place to pluck and devour its prey. It will not need to eat again for several hours. And the songbirds at my feeder will be scarce and wary for days to come.

Crows Home to Roost

It is 4:08 pm exactly as I sit by my front window on a chilly day late in November. The sun is now down behind the Black Hills and the clear cold light of almost-sunset fills the sky. As I look out the window, I see the first crow. It is flapping with purpose, working its way on a straight path southwest. Its glossy black feathers gleam as they pick up the last slanted rays of sunlight.

As it disappears from view, a few more crows appear in a group: the same strong purposeful flight all headed in the same direction. As I watch over the next fifteen minutes, a stream of crows passes over the house, a glossy black ribbon headed off to bed and to roost for the night. This is how crows spend their nights: they find a communal roost tree, high above the city streets.

Roosting is a word that is used for how birds rest and sleep. Many birds pass the dark hours of the night alone: the varied thrush that works the day shift scratching out grubs from under the fallen leaves in my backyard will find a thick shrubby bush in which it spends the night alone.

Birds of the blackbird family, which includes crows, like to hang out together at night. It is not well understood why they do this. Possible reasons include protection from predators: many eyes are available to watch for danger. Or perhaps they like the social aspects of hanging out with black-feathered kith and kin. We do not know.

From my observations, crows usually choose tall conifer trees in which to roost. They seem to like areas in which several conifers are clustered together and they seem to prefer areas near water. When we lived on Trosper Lake, we became familiar with the roost trees used by a large flock of starlings (also in the blackbird family). Each night they chose different trees, perhaps dependent on temperature and wind direction. It is theorized that certain parts of a given roost tree offer better protection at night and the dominant birds in the flock get to use these places. The lower ranking birds end up in the colder, more risky spots on the outside of the roost tree.

When the birds first arrive at the roost site, there is generally a lot of jostling and cawing and general mayhem, which is very noticeable to nearby humans. Sometimes you will see the crows shuffle and flop and move en masse from one tree to the next, a sort of Goldilocks dilemma in which they try to pick exactly the right bed.

As the light fades from the sky, the crows settle in and preen their feathers: this is important to help them hold in heat throughout the night. They sit and look out for awhile, shiny black eyes curious and watchful. Some may tuck their heads under their wings for a real sleep. But it seems that there is always at least one guard crow who stays awake enough to screech out a warning if warning is needed.

While the crows fly to roost every night, pretty much in the same fashion throughout the year, I always notice their goodbye to the sun more strongly in winter. Perhaps it is that these strings of crows flying off to bed are a powerful signal to the end of the day and the end of the light. And at 4:30 in the afternoon on a dark winter day, I am not quite ready to say goodbye to the light - or the birds.

The Aftermath: The Storms of December 1996

It is several days after the great ice storm of 1996 before I am able to go look at my favorite patch of woods along Dogtooth lane. This is a wet area dominated by Red Alder, Cascara and Bigleaf Maple; now most of the trees are broken off, split down the trunk, their branches on the ground. Tears stand in my eyes as I look at the destruction.

I am not alone. The silver thaw was a storm that all of us will remember. The writers of our local newspaper are not usually known for poetry, but in writing about this storm, they called it the night of breaking trees. A friend of mine whose people have walked this land for generations before the first settlers showed up said that on the night of the storm she heard the spirits of the trees screaming in the icy woods. On that night another friend had to put in ear plugs because the sounds of dying trees also broke her heart.

And yet: Nature does not create forests for our needs. Nature can send a silver thaw and destroy trees and we have nothing to say in the matter. And the terrible beauty of this storm aside, it can also provide benefits to the forest that are not immediate apparent to human eyes.

There are already some suggestions of how the forest may benefit from this storm. Work crews with their wood chippers are already out in the forests taking the dead wood and creating piles of wood chips. Within those piles, the spores of Morel mushrooms are dancing, sending out tiny white mycelia and preparing for a really fine crop of spring mushrooms.

The red alders have always had the special ability of extracting nitrogen from air and storing it in nodules in their roots. Now the dying trees release that nitrogen to the soil, enriching the fertility of the forest and making it possible for other plants to prosper.

Up in the canopy, the broken tree tops have opened up new holes for the sunlight to pour through. In the understory new generations of plants take advantage of these light-filled openings and start their own race towards the sun.

Down in the wetlands along Dogtooth Lane, the beavers find a treasure trove of alder branches on the ground. They will drag these branches to their water-logged den and peel the bark for winter food. They will use the leftovers to shore up their dams, blown out in the storm. For them, a silver thaw can go a long way to improving the quality of their winter life.

Other animals also teach me about the aftermath of storms. In our yard stretches out the 30 foot corpse of a Port Orford cedar, which under the weight of the ice broke out from its split leader. Along its newly opened trunk, a Ruby-crowned kinglet hops, gleaning minute insects from the exposed bark. Varied thrushes grub out in the shrubby mess under the tree, foraging for food. The black-capped chickadees pick through the lichens for winter food.

There are new spar trees created, broken off stubs of trees into which woodpeckers will carve their nest holes. And in my friend's neighborhood, a spar tree created an open, comfortable perch for a red-tailed hawk, the first time in many years such a bird has been seen in her area.

The ice storm was followed by a Chinook, a blast of warm wet wind coming up from the south that makes the temperatures soar high into the 50's. I walk again along Dogtooth Lane and am comforted, seeing the salmonberry's early green buds and tiny magenta flowers on hazel making their first appearance. The red elderberry buds grow swollen and fat and the skunk smell of Indian plum sap rising is prevalent throughout the wetland.

And I learn again that Nature makes up for her storms in the coming of spring and the promise of recovery and regrowth.

A Night in Garfield Ravine

It was just after sunset on a cold clear night in February when we decided to go down into the ravine behind our house and listen for owls.

We bundled ourselves up in our winter woolies and carried binoculars in mittened hands. We stood for a while and quieted ourselves down, our ears tuned up for the calls of one of the common yet elusive backyard birds. When we were finally ready, we filed down into one of Olympia's many neighborhood ravines to listen for owls.

Though this particular ravine is in the middle of residential Olympia, it still retains a rich mix of big leaf maples, alders and second-growth conifers. It has steeply pitched sides, so no houses have ever been built into it. The stream that once ran freely through this part of Olympia is now locked away in culverts underground, but here in the ravine it is once again open and running free into Puget Sound.

The stream probably carved out the deep ravine in times past. Now with recent rains, the water level was high and we listened to the rushing sound over the rocks in the creek bed. High up in the ravine, the wind brushed through winter-bare tree branches and the distant voices of children at play in the neighborhoods around the ravine floated down to our ears.

As expected in February, the ravine was cold and wet. But it was also waking slowly to spring and new life.

It was the perfect place for owls.

We sat and let the silence flow into us. We sat and let the night darken and the stars come out one by one. And then the owl began to call.

A quiet rolling series of hoots echoed up the ravine towards us. A haunting sound, the hollow heartbeat of the night woods, it came towards us. We held our breath and cupped our ears into radar dishes as we strained to hear. And it called again.

For the next hour, the Western Screech Owl asserted its claim to the ravine, as its kind had done for centuries. We sat, entranced, and let the sound fill us up. Up in the neighborhoods people went about their usual Sunday evening lives and missed the call. But for us in the ravine, we were blessed with the presence of owls.

Spring

Shorebirds Begin Their Migration

It was late March and the shorebirds were beginning to migrate through our area. Leaving the wintering grounds in the estuaries of Puget Sound, they head north to the tundra of Alaska and Canada, where they will mate, breed and raise young. Others are coming from the south and just passing through our area. I decided to go out to Kennedy creek, a pocket estuary on Totten inlet in southern Puget Sound, to watch the show.

That morning it was sunny but cold, with a biting north wind. I parked my car along a wayside on Kamilche Point road. It had a sweeping view of the tidal mudflats and the sun shone through breaks in the tree canopy overhead.

I pulled out my campstool and spotting scope and leaned against the car, using it as a windbreak. The dark color of the car had picked up some warmth from the sun and it was a welcome sensation against my back. Up the road, there were people staying warm by their wood stoves, enjoying their Sunday morning rituals. But I huddled in my coat and turned my face and scope to the estuary to watch one of nature's great spectacles.

Shorebirds are animals whose lives are intimately intertwined with the tidal estuary. They make a living by using their bills to winkle out marine invertebrates that live in rich mud: tiny shrimp, little clams and polychaete worms.

These tiny creatures live in the tidal flats and time their daily activity to the rise and fall of the tide. Shorebirds rely on the tides to bring this prey closer to the surface where it can be readily found by probing bill or quick eye. As the tide rises, the shorebirds get much more active and the pace of the feeding frenzy quickens.

At Kennedy Creek, there were several birds in the process of getting ready for breeding season in the high Arctic. The black-bellied plovers were molting their worn winter feathers to dapper summer plumage and looked very handsome in their dazzling black bellies and tweed-flecked backs. They prowled their sandy territories and quickly drove off any other birds impertinent enough to challenge them.

The dunlins were out in force, the dull browns of winter plumage molting to bright russet backs and startling black belly patches against pure white.

The killdeer prowled restlessly over the mudflats, their piercing K-DEE K-DEE K-DEE acting as a warning call for all the birds to get their heads up and look for trouble, say in the form of a hunting peregrine falcon.

And when alarmed, the shorebirds bolt up from the mudflats almost as one animal, shrilling warnings and forming flocks, moving and twisting in a kind of aerial ballet, their underparts flashing white and then dark in an attempt to confuse the predator.

But that day at Kennedy Creek, there was no predator, only one human slowly getting chilled on her campstool.

The sun got stronger and I watched the tide push the shorebirds into my view. I listened to the sound of the wind in the trees and the mournful call of the plovers drifting across the flats.

The sun glistened on the water and the creek swelled with the incoming tide. The force of the moon pulled the tide back into Totten inlet and also pulled the shorebirds into my Sunday morning devotions.

Hawk Migration at Bahokus Peak

Each spring in the Pacific NW, bird migration begins in subtle ways. Flocks of robins gather along roadsides, turning over matted leaves to search for grubs. Varied thrushes form groups under the evergreen trees and flights of migrating swallows skitter high in the sky as they vanish to the north. Rufous hummingbird males show up early, just in time for the salmonberry and red-flowering currant to put on a floral and nectar feed.

And along the coastline of Washington State, hawks of all kinds begin to move north, using the lines of coast and mountains as a compass to orient them on their journey. Eventually the hawks run out of land, getting bottled up at the large funnel that is Cape Flattery. With ocean to the west and the Straits of Juan de Fuca in front of them to the north, they have to decide how to cross fifteen miles of cold salt water. They wait and watch for good weather; eventually the right conditions occur and so begins one of the most exciting spring spectacles in western North America.

On a warm day in the first week of April, with sunny conditions and an east wind moving along the Strait, the hawks ready themselves for the big jump over the water to Canada. I join the hawks by going up to Bahokus, a hilltop that rises 800 feet above the town of Neah Bay.

From Bahokus, on a clear day I can see Vancouver island to the north, the Strait of Juan de Fuca at my feet, the little town of Neah Bay curled into a sandy spit and the Pacific Ocean to the south, all the way to Cape Alava and beyond. As the sun hits my hilltop, air currents called thermals are created. These consist of a slow whirlpool of air that revolves and rises several hundred feet in the air. The hawks are expert at finding and using these thermals. They get on the edge of one, set their wings to glide and ride the thermal elevator as much as 3000 feet+. When the thermal gets high enough, it cools and breaks apart and the elevator ride comes to an end. The hawks then set their wings and begin a long slow descent, gliding across the miles of water to Canada.

This use of the thermal elevator is a very efficient migration strategy for hawks, allowing them to conserve their energy. It also creates a wonderful spectacle for human visitors to watch.

Today on Bahokus, thermals start to form about 8:30 am. Out of the trees from below my viewpoint, the hawks start to rise. They lazily test out the air currents and watching each other carefully, they wait for a good thermal. When one hawk hits the jackpot, the others race over and try to catch a ride as well. As the thermal gains strength, a formation of hawks called a kettle form. It looks like a just-stirred soup pot, with swirling currents full of chunks of hawk.

A typical kettle at Cape Flattery has 50 hawks. These are mostly adult red-tailed hawks, whose slow stately flaps and brown-red tails define this species. Another common migrant is the sharp-shinned hawk; these are smaller and darker against the blue sky and look like tiny biplanes. Bald and golden eagles also use the thermals: they like to preserve their energy as much as possible, so they soar for long periods on long, flat, black wings. The falcons such as peregrines and merlins are the Olympic athletes of the hawk world and don't need thermals. They shoot right over my head and fly with powerful strokes straight for the coast of Canada.

For the volunteers on Bahokus, our job is to count and identify the hawks. On one remarkable day at the hilltop, we had three active thermals going all day. By the end of that day we had counted 3800 hawks making the northern crossing.

In all my years of nature watching, that may be the best day yet. I went to bed that night and when I closed my eyes, images of hawks were etched on my retinas and flew through my dreams. And in my memory, they are still flying…

Mima Mound Prairies Set Seed

Along the southern edges of the Puget sound trough, the Mima Mound prairies lie quietly in the afternoon sun.

In my memory, I am just weeks away from high school graduation. My friend and I are hiking through the Black Hills and stumble across the lands destined to become a Department of Natural Resources park. Though at that age fairly oblivious to nature, we were struck dumb by the powerful beauty & mystery of these grasslands.

The land here has been pushed up into rounded mounds, some ten feet high and fifteen feet across. These mounds march across the landscape for miles. No one knows how they were formed. We do know that they mark the southern extent of the last Ice Age, some 10,000 years ago. The plow-like edge of the glacier pushed enormous piles of gravel called glacial till and left it in huge piles at the southern terminus of the glacier. Perhaps this created the conditions that formed these mounds.

The gravel that covers these mounds also defines the plants that live here; though these grasslands receive the same 55 inches of water that southern Puget sound receives, here that water runs quickly through the thin soils and away out the watershed. The plants that can survive these conditions are more properly found in the desert lands of eastern Washington State. These prairies with their unusual geology, plant and animal communities are found no place else on the North American continent.

Today on our visit, the Idaho fescue was green and tall in the spring afternoon, the grass blades restless in the erratic wind, gusting down from the Black Hills. Camas flowers nodded bluely from erect stalks. Shooting star, kinnickinnick, bracken fern, lomatium, delphinium and spring sunshine: a host of native plants rose out from between clumps of the fescue bunchgrass and clamored for our attention.

We picked one Mima mound and sat quietly there, listening to the wind sough through the surrounding fir trees and run ripples across the prairie grass. It was an afternoon out of time, full of mystery and a beauty beyond words. I did not know it then, but seeds were planted in me that afternoon: a love of these prairies and a fascination with their unique grass, wildflowers and butterflies that would later blossom in my life.

We were not the only people to value these lands. The indigenous peoples used many of the plants for food and medicine. Camas bulbs were a main food crop and useful in barter with tribes throughout the Northwest. Prior to the coming of the settlers, the native people regularly burned the prairies to encourage the growth of the food plants. These seasonal burns discouraged woody invaders like Douglas fir and also returned fertility to the thin soils. In many ways, these prairies were like agricultural fields to the native peoples. They had a real talent of allowing the prairies to flourish while also meeting their own food and medicine needs.

Since the coming of the Euro-American settlers, the prairies have lain fallow. Since there have been no fires, non-native grasses, Scots broom and trees have invaded. A more insidious attack has been the boom in development in this area. It took nature many thousands of years to create these prairies; once destroyed we humans do not have the grasp of nature to be able to restore them.

Fortunately, there are winds of change in the prairies. Groups such as the Nature Conservancy are working hard to protect these lands. One local community group called Friends of the Prairies gathers each year, to celebrate these special places, to teach others about their importance and to ensure that future high school kids will have access once again to such remarkable places.

The Swirling of the Swifts

It was two weeks ago in late April that a friend called to tell me about a group of Vaux's Swifts that was roosting in a chimney near the state Capitol in Olympia. I was eager to check this out; when I arrived there the next evening near dusk, nearly fifty people were gathered on the lawn in front of one house, waiting for the swifts to perform their remarkable nightly ritual.

Around 8:30 pm, small flocks of swifts suddenly appeared, gathering over one specific house with a large-mouthed, open brick chimney. More and more dark specks of swallow-like birds appeared, fluttering and twittering over our heads. We estimated 400 birds. The flock moved restlessly to and fro across the darkening sky.

As the evening wore on, they started moving in thick swirling circles around the chimney itself. They formed a ribbon-like pattern in their flight. The circle grew tighter and tighter, as if the birds were caught up in a cyclone.

Finally, one part of the ribbon of swifts detached from the group, right above the chimney. Individual birds then stalled out their flight, and fell like large autumn leaves, tumbling backwards into the chimney.

This was the signal to the rest of the swifts; within a few minutes all of the swifts were safely at roost for the night, deep in the chimney. One scout bird stayed out and flew around to gather up the latecomers until all the birds disappeared within the chimney. When all were safely inside, the human observers politely applauded the show.

Vaux's swifts are insect-eating birds that look and behave much like swallows but in fact are more closely related to hummingbirds. They spend the winter down in the warmer climates of Central and South America where insect prey is more prevalent, but return to the Pacific Northwest to breed. They migrate in flocks and they like to roost together at night. They have very strong feet and claws; at night they use these feet to cling inside of hollowed out tree snags. But the changes in habitat wrought by humans have meant that snags are few and far between, so some swifts have adapted to using chimneys.

The flock we saw in the Capitol neighborhood was no doubt a group of swifts that had been migrating together. The weather had been cold and wet, so the birds were not yet eager to begin nesting or even to migrate further north.

A few blocks away from the chimney roost was the Deschutes estuary. I speculated that this group of birds was using the nearby estuary as a rich source of aerial insects. At night they rose up the hill from the estuary and sought out the nearest approximation to a snag that they could use for their night time roost. This probably occurs every year; the previous year I had heard of a different house that had hosted a migratory flock of swifts.

As the days warm up and the insect blooms begin I expect the swifts will leave the migration group and form breeding pairs, seeking out individual nest sites. In fact one of our friends called us about a nesting swift pair in her house last year.

For three weeks she'd been disconcerted because the adult birds were bringing live insects to the clamoring young in the chimney nest. Occasionally some of the insects escaped the gaping maws and made their way into the house. It was pretty noisy too: the hatchlings scratched and hollered for food throughout the daylight hours. But after three weeks, the young birds fledged and left the chimney for good. They did not return the next year.

Come fall, the swifts will group up once against and make their way south. But I look forward to next April and the return of the swifts as a harbinger of beautiful summer days ahead.

Swallow Season

It was in early May that I sat on the grass by our garden, reveling in one of the first definitively warm days of spring. The sun baked the eastern wall of the house, reflecting the heat through my shirt and also into the soil. As I troweled out the dirt, I suddenly noticed a small herd of violet-green swallows swoop into the neighborhood. The warm weather had triggered their urge to seek a place to nest.

As I sat and watched, the swallow band flew in large circles around the block. They were flying at a height of about 12 feet, close to the eaves of the houses. Occasionally one swallow would stop to check out a promising opening in the wood. They seemed to have a specific search image in mind for the best nest site, much as a human in the mall seeks out that one particular sweater. For the next fifteen minutes I watched as the swallows circled and searched my block and then into the next block in what appeared to be a systemic exploration for nest cavities.

Before the loggers appeared in western Washington, violet-green swallows nested in cavities in old-growth trees. Today there is a serious lack of old growth trees and the accompanying nest holes, so nesting sites are at a premium. Violet green swallows have adapted somewhat, using whatever holes they can find, including holes in the metal pipes that hold the traffic lights. We can also provide housing for them: specially designed swallow boxes placed high on a sunny wall will be very acceptable. We have such a box on our house and pairs of swallows fight vociferously each year to see who gets to use it.

Last year our box was used by a pair who successfully raised three fledglings. After the noisy battles for the house, things quieted down. The first signs of serious nesting included small bits of moss and grasses dropped in the garden below the box. The birds also plucked out their own breast feathers to line the grass nest, so often we would see a few white feathers trapped in the rosemary bush underneath.

After nest building is completed things really get quiet and it appears the box is deserted. Not so: eggs have been laid and the pair takes turns incubating the eggs, slipping in and out of the box in a sneaky changing of the guard. After about 2 weeks they hatch and we stand under the box and listen for the first delicate cheeps of the hatchlings. The tiny birds grow prodigiously over the next three weeks; their delicate calls turn to outright squalls and shrill shrieks as they clamor for food. Around the 4th of July they will fledge, taking that first risky flight into independent life. It doesn't look like an easy choice: the parents have to lure them out of the box with food and repeated demonstrations of flight technique. It takes the young birds a while to make the commitment.

One of my favorite nature watching activities is to spend some time with the young birds just before they fledge. One sunny afternoon late in June I set up a spotting scope and comfortable chair some distance from the box and watched the young swallows. Three baby heads all competed for space at the open slot in the nest box as they watched their parents search for food. They were so alert, their bright dark eyes constantly searching the sky for parental food units. But they were also wary and careful; when a crow flew by they hastily retreated into the depths of the box. Somehow, even at that young age, they knew that crows were a serious danger.

They were molting into adult plumage so the feather patterns on each bird were distinctive. One was clearly the bully of the bunch, taking over most of the space at the nest hole and shouldering others out of the way when parents arrived with food. Vocal, very active, very noisy, they kept me company much of that summer afternoon. It was a real joy.

A few days later, the swallows had left the box. I didn't see the final exit; I think now that the young birds fledge under cover of early morning, when they are less likely to be snatched by crows. Most likely the family moved down the hill to the Deschutes estuary where they will spend the rest of the summer learning the insectivore trade. They will figure out the tricky business of catching bugs on the wing and will lay down fat stores for the long migration south.

But come next March, when a warm Chinook wind blows through and the days warm up, flocks of violet green swallows will come winging over the horizon and back into our summer lives.

Summer

Return of the Bumblebees

It was a cold morning in late May and we had grumpily decided it was time to clear out our weed-choked flower beds. It had been rainy much of the previous week but that day warmed up to about 55 degrees. We wandered around the garden, making feeble attempts at pulling the biggest weeds, leaving piles of freshly upturned soil behind.

It was then that we noticed a big, black solitary bumblebee sharing the garden with us. She ignored us but was very interested in the newly turned soil, landing on the shallow clumps and carefully exploring these. We watched this behavior on and off all afternoon.

It was only later when I checked a resource book on insects that I realized that this was a queen Bombus vosnesenkii or Yellow-faced bumblebee. She is a ground-nesting bee and she was looking for a place to build her nest. Typically she seeks out an abandoned mouse, mole or gopher burrow. Probably the scent of the fresh soil got her thinking that there was a good nesting site in our garden.

Once she finds a suitable site, she will create a waxy ball and lay eggs into individual larval cells. She will sit on her eggs and incubate them much as a bird incubates her eggs. She will make occasional forays out for nectar and pollen and then return to her brood. After about four weeks, the first bees will emerge. These are the workers and they take over the work of the hive, foraging for nectar and pollen The queen becomes an egg laying machine and in about three months her life will end, deep in her hive in the earth. She is unlikely to see the sky again.

Bumblebees of the insect tribe Bombini are extremely important native pollinators of our early spring and summer crops. They are able to work in much colder temperatures than the non-native honey bees whose genetic tolerance to cold was developed in warmer Mediterranean climates. Bumblebees seem somewhat less prone to the disease currently plaguing honey bees.

And bumblebees have always been here; their genetic design makes them perfectly suited to the pollination of our native plants. I am always delighted to welcome bumblebees back to our gardens each year.

Last April a friend had put up a bird box but was very disappointed that no birds came along to use it. She started to think that bumblebees might have taken it over, which would discourage any bird. So we waited until night time temperatures had dropped below 50; even bumblebees have trouble staying active then. We carefully opened up the bird box and pointed our flashlight inside. We were astounded to see the box half full of carefully shredded moss; perhaps 25 sleepy bumblebees crawled slowly around the moss, trying to get away from the light. It was an amazing window into the lives of these bees. After a few minutes we quietly closed the box and left them to their sleep.

By August, the hives are bustling and the bees take advantage of every moment of sun to forage for their nest. This became clear to me as I visited a friend who had designed a pollinator garden specifically to attract bees and butterflies. Her garden in August was a cornucopia of Cosmos, Lavender and Catmint, Black-eyed Susans and Bee Balm, all displaying their flowers like laying out wares at the market. The bumblebees were the main customers that day. We watched and counted at least six different species., and hundreds of bees, foraging in her garden.

As we stood and listened to their buzzings, we felt the last days of summer sun on our faces. I remember that day now like a farewell to summer; us and the bees soaking up the last bit of sun to carry us through the darker months ahead.

High Summer

Here in the end of July, it is now high summer. As I move through this season, I see the tentative spring green leaves of the deciduous trees have now reached full outstretched green bloom, competing for every millimeter of sunlight. I can almost hear photosynthesis and the rush of carbohydrates down the tree trunks to be stored in the roots for winter. The shrubs too are part of the show: the bare spaces in the woods are now stuffed full of shrubby leaves, covering the scars of the winter's ice storm. No longer is there any bare soil: the open ground of winter is now hidden by a profusion of herbaceous plants, each making sure no patch of ground remains open. And the gold-green grasses: all reach skyward, their fluffy bloom heads swaying and shining under the hot summer sun. Everywhere in summer, the grasses are king.

The sky has a particular blue luminance in high summer: a shimmering blue that seems to go on forever. The meteorologists describe this as an unlimited ceiling. Fat puffs of clouds float across from the north, which is where the best weather of high summer comes from.

The water of Puget Sound has a particular quiet midnight blue quality in summer. Even as the tide rushes in and out, the surface of the bay is quieter, with occasional riffles that change the texture.

And the animals of high summer are active. The birds are done with nesting and now are busy stuffing fledgling maws full of wriggling insects. You can see it on your lawn: the constant yammering of the young, the begging behavior, the frantic parents trying to find enough food to shut them up. Out in the prairie meadows, the fritillary butterflies are now emerging from chrysalids hidden deep in the violets. Soon the meadows will be full of large orange butterflies nectaring on the abundant thistle flowers of high summer.

And yet, high summer is a season that ebbs and flows. I remember sitting one late July day many years ago on the steps of the old Wash Tub laundromat on Harrison hill. I was with my sister, and we sat outside that afternoon, looking down the hill towards the bay and Mount Tahoma. As the afternoon wore on, we sat and talked of many things and watched the summer afternoon unfold. The tide floated out, and we smelled the strong rich scent of the estuary. The mountain was impossibly beautiful that day, and most of the winter's snow was melted. As I sat there, the shadows lengthening in the afternoon, I saw the rich translucent blue of the sky deepen in the darker blue of early fall. The heat of the day seemed to seep away, and I felt the first hint of fall chill in the air. For the first time in my life, I understood that summer was a tide, flowing in flowers and grasses and baby birds and blue skies and hot sun. On that day, sitting on the steps, I watched the tide come in, slacken and start to turn. And I knew that high summer was on its way out.

Salmon Complete their Journey

Salmon are returning once again to our streams.

This event, once a cause of great celebration by native people is met by us immigrants today in quieter fashion. The return is signaled by crowds hanging out on the 5th Avenue bridge in Olympia, where Capitol Lake drains into the salt waters of Budd inlet. Normally people use this bridge only as a path to someplace more important. But when the salmon run in the estuary, people stop to watch, to drool and to marvel.

The first fish to show up are the Chinook, or King salmon. After several years at sea, they return to spawn in the upper reaches of the Deschutes river. On arrival in the Straits of Juan de Fuca they are a bright silvery color. But as they move south, into the brackish waters of their home estuary, their body chemistry changes to adapt to fresh water. They also change into a kind of "breeding plumage" much as birds do. Sockeye salmon shift from bright silver to a scarlet red that glows vividly in the murky waters of the bay. Dog salmon males develop a pronounced canine hook to their upper jaws, the better to compete with and terrorize other males. All these changes prepare salmon for the final act of their lives.

.At the 5th avenue bridge, Chinook and Silver salmon provide the main show. They are not native to this river/estuary: there are big falls on the lower river which blocked salmon passage until the construction of a fish ladder around 1955. After its construction the river was planted with hatchery Chinook and Silver, though I have also seen wandering Sockeye and Pinks trying to kick their way out of the holding pens at the Deschutes hatchery.

After the salmon arrive in the estuary, they feed in preparation for the move upstream to the spawning grounds. Their urge to run is triggered by the first heavy fall rains, but at Budd inlet they must wait for the right tides and an open dam. One can almost sense their restlessness at such times. Once I stood on the bridge and watched several big Chinook waiting for the dam to open. They circled fitfully around the inlet and seemed to be exploring the shoreline for another opening upstream. They were so large I had an uneasy sensation of SHARK. It was near sunset : the quality of bronze light cast an otherworldly feel to the salt water as round and round the big salmon cruised, dorsal fins cutting fishy tracks on the surface of the bay.

The people who watch the show are an assortment. There are the fisherman lusting for the opening of the season and bitching about the harbor seals who seem to be stealing "their" fish. There are those people who love to eat salmon: you can almost see them drool as they watch. There are parents who take their kids to the bridge like they are going to the zoo.

And there are those who go for celebration: for another year, the salmon have succeeded and have returned to the estuary and to us…

Caterpillars

Here in early September, the sun is still beating down strongly in these last dying days of summer. This is a time when many animals are dashing around, flying around, crawling around taking advantage of summer to prepare for harder days to come.

So one day I am sitting out on the patio, basking in the sunshine and enjoying the flowers we have planted to attract butterflies to our garden. Suddenly my eyes are drawn to tiny movements on the late-blooming fennel. When I go to investigate, I find a pair of Anise Swallowtail caterpillars marching up and down the flower stems, chowing down on the polls-rich spikes. I was enthralled.

At some point a few weeks ago, an adult Anise Swallowtail must have visited our garden. Besides using the nectar flowers to feed, she was also looking for her preferred host plants in which to lay her eggs. She will only use plants in the carrot family and especially likes dill, fennel and carrot tops. She lays minute single green eggs somewhere on the stem. After about two weeks the tiny caterpillars chew their way out of the egg sac and start eating the fennel. Thus was my garden gifted by caterpillars.

Each day we go out and check their progress. They are truly gorgeous: fat and succulent, with vivid green, black and yellow stripes. When they sense our presence, they freeze up on the stem and play dead. But if sufficiently provoked, they arch up and push out bright orange horns from their heads, making them look fearsome indeed.

As we watch them over the next ten days, they eat prodigiously, growing visibly bigger each day. At some point their skin can stretch no further. At that point they stop eating, find a quiet spot and molt the old skin, pushing it off like pulling off a dirty sock. Then they start eating again with renewed and even more voracious appetite.

Our swallowtail caterpillars go through three molts or instars. After the third instar, they are huge; maybe one and a half inches long. They are frantically eating and the results are visible on the ragged fennel. After several days of this behavior, they stop eating and get very restless. They start a constant moving, going on what we call walkabout. At this time they are looking for a safe place to go through their final molt into a chrysalis.

When the caterpillars in our garden went on walkabout, we lost track of them. But we know that somewhere in the butterfly garden, they looked for a sturdy branch They crawled up, cast a silken line about themselves to be anchored firmly in place, hung upside down by their bottommost pair of feet and cast off their last skin. In 24 hours, a brown sack-like chrysalis will be firmly attached to the stick. To our eyes, it will look like a dead leaf.

But inside the chrysalis, the genetic code of the swallowtail is at work, keeping it alive and dormant in a winter holding pattern. Through several months of rain, ice and snow, the chrysalis will keep the butterfly safe.

Sometime next March, after a week of sun and warmer temperatures, genetic codes, magic & life itself will stir. The inchoate goo inside the chrysalis will miraculously transform into a butterfly. The butterfly will break open the stiff brown walls of the chrysalis and will crawl out to another season. And next year's Anise Swallowtail butterflies will take flight in our garden once again.

Legacies

On November 5, 1997, my grandmother Helen died. She was 96 years old.

We received the call at 3:15 am and drove out to the hospital for one last visit. I will remember that drive all my life. It was a full moon night, the one that some call Snow Moon. It shone starkly beautiful at times on that drive to the hospital, and other times obscured by dense, cold fog.

The road to the hospital crossed over Budd Inlet, where a very full tide lapped at the pilings of Percival Landing. When we returned home an hour later, the tide had turned, pulling strongly to the north and I knew it took my Grandma's spirit with it.

My grandma Helen grew up on an isolated homestead on Jewel Lake in northern Idaho. This was in 1905 and they had very few neighbors in this rugged country. Throughout the days of her childhood she ran wild over those hills, learning to know every plant and tree, every animal, every inch of our her own natural world.

And it was her legacy to me to show me that world She took me to the mountains where we hiked the Plains of Abraham near Mt. St. Helens. She showed me the beauty of Indian Paintbrush, Lupine and Bear-grass in a mountain meadow. I remember standing with her at Windy Pass just below Mt. St. Helens where she showed me the five great Cascade volcanoes: Baker, Tahoma, Adams and Hood, all visible together in that one place on earth.

She took me to her brother's place on the bay at Little Tykle Cove. Here at low tide the estuary stretched out before us, its rich abundant life a nursery for southern Puget Sound. Here were Lewis' Moonshells, big snails we pulled with sucking sounds out of the gloppy mud. Here were thick coalescing beds of sand dollars and dangerous squirting clams.

She took me to the ocean where she shared her love of the sound of crashing waves. I learned to watch birds there: the skitter of sanderlings along the water's edge and the ponderous flight of pelicans. We explored tide pools together and together we were fascinated by sea anenomes, sea urchins and hermit crabs.

In the last years of her life, we switched roles and I took her on a few trips. We went to the San Juan Islands to watch the Orca whales as they swam by on their daily patrols for salmon. Last winter on a rare sunny day we sat along Budd inlet and watched the winter ducks. She was like a child again in her wonder and joy.

This summer we took one final trip back to Jewel Lake, Idaho. It was not much changed; she stood by her favorite old fishing hole and looked one more time upon this beloved place. She knew again every species of tree, every water plant, every bird. And this time, because of her, I knew them too. Because of her gifts to me, I recognized the Ponderosa pines, the native pond lily choking one shallow corner of the lake and the sharp rachety call of the hunting kingfisher.

Perhaps it was then that we both knew that her legacy to me was nearly complete.

My Life as a Naturalist

I didn't set out to become a naturalist. In fact for a long time I didn't even know what that word meant (a dictionary search reveals: a naturalist is a student of nature and natural history). That seems to be very accurate for me. I am a student and I will always be learning, especially about the complex natural world around us.

I started my official journey in 1985 when I decided to learn about birds. I went on birding expeditions with my friend Denny Granstrand in the Yakima valley of eastern Washington state and from there it all unfolded.

I followed my nose to exploring marine mammals, especially watching gray whales on the Oregon coast. I moved back over the mountains to Puget Sound and volunteered at Point Defiance Zoo as a zookeeper aide, working alongside some phenomenal biologists like Margaret Gaspari who opened my eyes to the world of bats.

Later I assisted her in bat research project at Woodard Bay's bat colony and together we went to Arizona to attend a field workshop on bats with Merlin Tuttle.

From there I went to Massachusetts and took the Field Biologist training program offered at Manomet Bird Observatory on the coast south of Plymouth. That experience was one of those watershed moments in my life; it really deepened my understanding of the world of birds and many other creatures as well. While in Massachusetts I spent a week at Tom Brown's Wilderness Survival School, which had profound effects on my vision as a nature watcher.

I returned to Puget Sound and got interested in butterflies. By now I knew the best way to learn was to find a top teacher and learn from that person. For butterflies, I met Robert Pyle and took several workshops from him as I learned about our native butterfly species. From his wife Thea I especially learned about the host plants they require. The book Butterflies of Cascadia is a fabulous resource of all we need to know about butterflies in our bioregion.

By this time I had met my husband Glen, who is a landscape gardener. In sheer self-defense I had to learn about plants so as to keep up with him. I took botany with Laine McLaughlin at South Puget Sound Community College where she had a special focus on native plants. I bless her and her teachings to this day.

Since 1990 I have lived in Olympia, in close proximity to The Evergreen State College. Here I was able to learn from a number of excellent faculty. Jeff Cederholm taught me about Salmonid Ecology and David Milne about Salt marsh Ecology.

Throughout all this I volunteered at a number of great places. I worked at Nisqually Wildlife Refuge on kestrel nest box research and also band-tailed pigeons and their unique use of mineral springs. Recently I volunteered with South Sound Estuary Association and participated in their Beach Naturalist training. I spent several days on the tidal estuaries this summer, sharing natural history with families visiting the beach.

At some point it became important to teach nature classes to other people. I developed classes on the First Forty Birds, Shorebirds and Owls. I also taught classes on bats, butterflies and our native pollinator animals. It was a privilege to share this world of nature with others just starting on their own paths as nature students.

I started writing about nature, volunteering as a staff writer for Green Pages, a local newspaper produced by South Puget Environmental Education Clearing House. About five years ago my husband Glen Buschmann, my sister Nancy Partlow and I began a nature blog called Bees, Birds & Butterflies. We found that writing about nature kept us in better contact with the all the things that were happening outside our doors.

So this is my story as a nature watcher so far. And we will see what the future brings...

2014